THE NEW CZECH POETRY

THE NEW CZECH POETRY

Jaroslav Čejka
Michal Černík
Karel Sýs

translated by Ewald Osers

BLOODAXE BOOKS

ISBN: 1 85224 066 0

First published 1988 by
Bloodaxe Books Ltd,
P.O. Box 1SN,
Newcastle upon Tyne NE99 1SN.

Bloodaxe Books Ltd acknowledges
the financial assistance of Northern Arts.

Typesetting by Bryan Williamson, Manchester.

Printed in Great Britain
by Bell & Bain Limited, Glasgow, Scotland.

Contents

Introduction

Jaroslav Čejka, born 1943, was involved, during and after his engineering studies, with experimental "studio theatre" and for a while worked as a stage-hand at one of the big theatres in Prague. He increasingly drifted into cultural and literary work, and in 1982, when *Kmen*, the literary supplement of the weekly *Tvorba*, was founded, became its first editor-in-chief. He started to publish his poetry in 1964, and although his work appeared in periodicals and in anthologies, his first independent volume *Sentimental Loves* did not appear until 1979. The title is meant ironically: the poetry is in fact quite unsentimental. His next volume, *Public Secret*, published in 1980, is largely a "private mirror" of a sadly ending and ended love affair – poetry captivating by the very absence of sentimentality and self-pity. While the first two books are written in a regular (though not classical) form with frequent rhymes, Čejka abandoned this style in his *Book of Requests and Complaints* and adopted a free verse – almost as if he wanted to lead the reader away from excessive concern with himself to concern with life and the world.

He went even further in that direction in his highly original next volume, his *Pocket Collection of Laws, Axioms and Definitions*, in which he applies the language of physical and other laws to human relationships. The gentle humour of this approach – which seems to owe something to Miroslav Holub – proved highly effective, largely because the basic natural laws used by Čejka are familiar to readers and are here suddenly applied, in a novel fashion, to a world of relationships and emotions normally beyond the scope of the natural sciences.

Michal Černík, born 1943, is the youngest poet to be honoured with the title 'Meritorious Artist', awarded to him in 1985. After extensive publication of his poetry in periodicals, his first volume, *Spare Landscape*, only appeared in 1971. The central part of this collection consists of monologues – by a stone, a jug, a rose, an apple, a mirror, a mountain, and the sky; all these reflect his intimate relationship with the landscape, the North Bohemian plain with the legendary Říp Hill rising from it. There is in his poetry a strong sense of family, or indeed clan, identity across the generations. Whereas, on the one hand, Černík's language is sparse, economical, there is, on the other, a tendency towards lengthy lyrical-epic cycles evoking the mystique of family and home. *Far is the Shadow, Far is the Garden* (1979) reflects his "generation relationship", his respect for the generations of his ancestors and his own, and his generation's, participation in the shaping of history.

While Černík's poetry for adults is marked by seriousness, and often *gravitas*, his children's verse (numerous volumes) as well as his prose for children and young readers, reveal a sense of humour and delight in play.

Černík has also translated Estonian and Lithuanian poetry, for anthologies published in 1977 and 1982, as well as – from literal translations by scholars – ancient Egyptian love lyrics (*Ancient Love Songs*, 1982).

Karel Sýs, born 1946, made his poetic début in a literary periodical in 1965. Even his early poetry bore the characteristics which were to emerge more clearly as his work matured – a sensuous language, direct and outspoken, full of enchantment with life and rejecting all hypocrisy and puritanism. His first volume of poetry, *Newton during the Failure of the Apple Crop*, came out in 1969. This was followed, in 1972, by *The Half-Open Angel*, a volume of playful imagery, strongly reminiscent of Rimbaud. For the next few years Sýs published only in periodicals, until in 1977 two new volumes of poetry appeared, *The Long Farewell* and *Take a Deep Breath and Fly*. The former, a deliberate echo of the title of Raymond Chandler's detective story, reflected Sýs's belief that Chandler and his Philip Marlowe probably knew more about the real America than did Hemingway. The latter of the two volumes was republished, in amplified form, in 1979.

By the early seventies Sýs's poetry had found a considerable circle of readers and was influencing some of the poets of his own and the next younger generation. In 1978 a selection of his love poems was published under the title *Carrier Pigeons of Memory* and in 1981 – when he was only 35 – a *Selected Poems*.

Karel Sýs has also translated a lot of poetry, mostly with the help of intermediary versions: from Hungarian, Mongolian, Bulgarian, Lithuanian, and especially French. Two volumes of translations from Apollinaire testify, as does his own poetry, to the affinity he feels for the French poet. Among Czech poets of an earlier generation it is mainly Vítězslav Nezval who has left a clear mark on Sýs's work. His *Time Machine* (1984) was hailed by reviewers as his best book so far.

Vladimír Janovic, born 1935, published his first poems in periodicals in 1962. His first volume, *Black-out of Paradise*, was published in 1968. Both it and his next book, *Romulus's Lamentation* (1970), reflect an existentialist sense of loneliness, senselessness and pointlessness.

By the time his next volume, *Honeycomb of Clay* (1975), appeared Janovic had arrived at a brighter, more active view of existence. His work not only contains a few baroque themes, but he also uses an increasing range of strict traditional forms, from the ghazal to the rondel.

As a kind of follow-up to the rondel 'Leningrad' from *Honeycomb of Clay* Janovic in 1978 published a cycle of twelve cantos, *Poem about a Snowy Levitation*, a highly successful poetical composition inspired by one of those magical "white nights" for which Leningrad is famous. It is, at the same time, a personal experience and a poetic awareness of the city of the Revolution, the city of the Blockade, the city of Peter the Great, Pushkin, Lenin, Blok and Akhmatova. The work is written in finely chiselled verse, in the tradition of the great pre-war Czech poets Vítězslav Nezval and Josef Hora. A very different book is his next volume of poetry, *Fair in the Mist*, whose individual poems are a kind of emotional biography of the author, from boyhood to adulthood. *All Your Bodies* (1983) revealed a power-fully sensual and erotic note in Janovic's poetry.

His close links with Italian culture and art are reflected in many of Janovic's poems, as well as by his translation of Cristofanelli's book on Michelangelo and his selection of Eisner's pre-war trans-lations of Michelangelo's poetry.

Most strongly, however, this "Italian side" of his artistic person-ality emerges from *The House of the Tragic Poet* (1984), a lyrical-epic – Janovic's description – poetic evocation of Pompeii a few days before its obliteration by volcanic ash from Mount Vesuvius. In his introduction to the book Janovic relates how, on looking at the mosaic floor in what is now (because of the mosaic) called the House of the Tragic Poet, he began to recreate in his mind the persons rep-resented in the mosaic and, as it were, bring them imaginatively to life. It is a quite remarkable achievement: the accuracy of archaeolog-ical detail combined with the sensitive recreation of the characters and the atmosphere lend the work a persuasiveness and a credibility that, heightened by Janovic's powerful poetic language, grip the reader almost as if he were reading a thriller. And it is not, of course, only about the last days of Pompeii: it is about real people, about human relationships, about life and death, and about tragic poetry as one of man's ways of coping with life and death.

EWALD OSERS

Jaroslav Čejka

Twelve Laws of the Heart

The Law of Gravitation

Two bodies attract one another with a force directly proportional
to the product of their masses and inversely proportional to
the square of the distance between them.

You weigh fifty-seven kilogrammes
I after my slimming diet a good eight-two
and the distance between us
is roughly three hundred kilometres
From this it can easily be calculated
that our mutual attraction
is 3.36×10^{-7} newtons
And that's not much
In physical terms it is
a negligible quantity

According to the law of gravitation we should
continue to move each in our own orbit
Except that on 3rd June this year
our paths crossed
And at a distance of a little under one metre
our mutual attraction increased
to over 30,000 newtons

Small wonder then that our bodies met
the first time on 9th June
(ten days after my father's death
a mere four after his funeral)
and then again and again
at ever shorter intervals

It was for us the Railways introduced
the Meridian, Istropolitan,
Hungaria, Thracia and the Slovak Arrow
It was for us the air traffic controllers
did not in spite of higher fuel costs
cancel Flights OK313   OK004 and others

Our paths underwent some strange correlations
They've long lost their elliptical shape

And yet we both of us know
that our flight equipment shows
some rather serious malfunctions

For who can tell if we shall ever return
from our flight with our skins intact
And who can tell whether and where and when
some cosmic accident awaits us
But since 19th January
nineteen eighty
we've now been flying side by side

At first in embrace
later arms linked
and finally supporting one another
Provided neither of us
gets into someone else's gravitational field
and provided neither of us
develops a tumour of indifference
at the intersection of the paths of reason and emotion
a tumour on which not even Professor Kunc
would wish to operate

Meanwhile Christmas is here
Three weeks to go till 19th January
And I'm engaged
in my calculations only
Because everything is relative

I have long been heavier by my mistakes
and by your love
which maybe I don't even deserve
And so
even if I'm in Prague for the time being
and you in Bratislava
I feel you standing behind me
looking over my shoulder and saying
        — In the gravitational constant
        you've got the order wrong

And I reply to you
that no constants apply
in love

The Law of Probability

Man proposes but sickness disposes
It is Saturday the 19th January
but in the Golden Hall of the Knights' Castle
the light and heating are off.

Our famous wedding is not taking place

You are pinned down by your gall-bladder's painful nails
to my orphaned bed
And I thanks to an eczema have scratched my way
to the Skin Ward of the Bulovka Hospital
from where I'm writing to you with fingers as yellow
as the late Chairman Mao

Man proposes but sickness disposes
Meanwhile I've no one to lean upon
and no one whose pain to make better by blowing on

Within a single year I lost my father
and my first wife
and slowly I am losing my children
But I realise that this doesn't interest anybody
What after all is one personal private crisis
against the latest crisis in the Middle East

Besides I don't want to bother anybody with it
I'm having my sickness benefit sent to my home
and my Party membership stamps are kept for me at work
My mail continues to go to my old-new address
I received twelve greeting cards for the New Year
My friends wish me good health and happiness and contentment
And wham
it's got me

I am content with my lot
After all by the laws of probability
I shouldn't be here at all

At age ten they predicted
that I wouldn't live to thirty
But here I am and I still cling to this world

Instead of a wedding suit of grey English cloth
I'm wearing an outsize yellowed institutional garment
But at least I'm not hot
and don't have to worry
about spilling coffee or red wine down my front

Man proposes but sickness disposes
Admittedly I have yellow fingers
but I am no great navigator
Outside the window it's snowing as in the Tibetan mountains
From afar comes the clatter of mysterious prayer wheels
But those are just the nurse's heels
as she lets down the blinds
on another winter's day

International love is a difficult business
Your gall-bladder couldn't take the assault of Czech pork
and my treacherous skin changed colour with the paprika
which is the hallmark of your cuisine
my *levelibéko*

It was a riotous New Year's Eve
You in bed
I in the armchair
with bandaged hands
But at midnight you rose
put on your pink dress from Budapest
and I my dinner jacket and over my bandages
I pulled on my white kid gloves
We toasted each other in champagne
lit sparklers
and I waited and wondered
if my children would ring

And you knew what I was waiting for
and after a long silence whispered
— I'll be a good wife to you

On New Year's Day I worked till two in the morning
And again from five
You made black coffee for me
and in the armchair behind me dried your hair with the hairdryer
There were a few things I didn't know then
and ignorance does not give rise to sin
whereas all knowledge faces us
with new decisions and new tasks

According to the law of probability
we should never have met
you a Hungarian from southern Slovakia
and I a Czech unbaptised by the Vltava

Except that we did meet
and that entails
certain risks

You call me *kisfiúcsko*
which in Hungarian means little boy
and little boys occasionally get lost
But I firmly believe
that I won't get lost with you
even though I've known for over a week
that you aren't mine alone

The Law of Natural Selection

The Balt-Orient Express which starts in Berlin
is already ninety minutes late on arrival in Prague
The engine driver's in no hurry to get anywhere
The engine driver is not getting married tomorrow
Unlike me

Some people have a lucky hand
in anything they do
My father was one of them
The horses in Chuchle

ran to his hopes
Fish swam to his hook
as if drugged
Mushrooms grew before his eyes
He always drew the right card in the end
And mother was quite right to love
his faults as well

Except that he left us
with no time to say goodbye
And I'm now scratching my head
over the question of correct selection
Selection of the fittest form of life
genuine values in art
and actions in politics
the best forest the right riverbed
comfortable shoes and uncomfortable friends
or even dishes from a menu

And there's selection and selection
Surely it matters
who is selecting whom or what   And why
For what purpose   Under what circumstances
And on what grounds

Racial characteristics appeal or origin
will not presumably be the right criteria
any more than pretended
zeal in faith

Moreover there are certain things on earth
that one simply can't choose for oneself
(among them for instance are
parents native land and one's own genes)
And others covered by the ancient saying
that He that chooses
often loses

And yet out of three million Czechoslovak women
of what is called child-bearing age
I've chosen you
It took me a long time

And it took us a good deal longer still
jointly to choose
our wedding menu

We had a skirmish
over entre soup aperitif
The laws of selection however are inflexible
The stronger one wins
And so you won

The Balt-Orient Express is just getting its breath back
under the vault of Brno station
And so am I between two great battles
Petrov is vanishing in the mist
And Špilberk is not yet visible

I make a note in my diary
that 15th February 1980 was a foggy day
with rain
I'm feeling like a victor
because at this time tomorrow
you'll be my own second wife
Even though it's quite possible
that this selection business was
the other way round

Archimedes' Principle

*When a body is immersed in a fluid it suffers a loss in weight
equal to the weight of fluid which it displaces*

Whereas a person entering into
the life of another
is displaced by the weight
of all memories habits and bad habits
for which there is suddenly no room left

Sometimes in your sleep you whisper
the names of strange men
and from my favourite books now and again
drops a photo of some face that doesn't age
in the same mirror
in which mine ages

In the year I first fell in love
you just started school
And in the year I first married
you first crossed
the bloody threshold of your own adolescence
Our two lives are displaced
against one another like the phases
of an electric current

My dead don't make you weep
But equally they won't ever
yield their place to you
And your first loves
even though they can no longer be jealous
will never take their perpetually critical
eyes off me

We're actors and spectators in a play
that has no end no middle and no beginning
We enter it in progress
from the proscenium the orchestra pit the trap
from the flies or the backdrop
and the play resists us like a body
into which a foreign body has suddenly entered

But this isn't a poem
about some limits of immunity
The body sometimes manages
to rid itself of a foreign body
But never a fluid

According to Archimedes' principle
a body in a fluid may
sink to the bottom
rise or float on the surface
But it can never fly up from it

I too cling like froth
to the surface of your breath
on which uneasily floats the trimaran of my heart
my body and my aching head
And I still don't know if in this
transatlantic race
we're aiming at first prize
or merely consolation

Pascal's Law

Pressure in a fluid is transmitted equally in all directions.

A fluid is not compressible
But the human soul is
And the nation's soul is so almost limitlessly

For three hundred years the Habsburgs squeezed
the soul of the Czech nation
until it fitted within the pages of the Kralice Bible
Six years the German Führer impressed
Böhmen und Mähren
on our Czech stamps
And the tiny Czech souls
collected political jokes
and courage
For many years the general
with the reflecting sunglasses squeezed
the throat of the woodcutter who awoke
in the presidential elections of 1970

For thirteen years I oppressed you
on our folding couch
and at the kitchen table
And only for twelve minutes
did I squeeze tears from my eyes
because in court it is embarrassing
to lose face

But the pressure in a fluid is transmitted in all directions
and with undiminished force
And that is why my tears erupted
on to the face of my new love
While the pressure which increased
in your heart like in a red Papin's pot
blew out the safety valves
of patience and habit
so that I suddenly found myself again at the beginning
Temporarily single practically childless
and with no material ties

Freedom is bought dearly
And sometimes you are conned
by skilful deceivers
You pay without receiving
honest goods
What's more the revolution just like love itself
no matter how well it behaves
succumbs after a while to the pressure
of colourless routine and everyday worries

Pascal's law cannot be avoided
But every pressure
gives rise to counter-pressure
and that's why I immunise my soul by poetry
against faintheartedness weariness and compliance

That's why I'll always defend you
my revolution
my love

The Law of Action and Reaction

Until age fourteen I was keen on fishing
At age fifteen sex gained the upper hand
At twenty-five I became addicted to art
and after thirty for a change to politics

And in all these I was successful

I loved a lot of beautiful women
who didn't love me
The biggest fish ever to bite
got away from my hook
For eighteen years I wrote poetry
before my first book was published
I have a lot of children
and even more debts
But every action produces a reaction
and so I now write poems like on a conveyor belt
I'm a member of six organisations
an expert on contraception
and the owner of a savings account
I've stopped believing in empty promises
life assurance
and happy endings

Every action produces a reaction
a fact well known to physicists gunners and revolutionaries
And reaction – just like money or fire –
is a good servant but a bad master
That of course is what man has a head and hands for
to check and direct every reaction
to force it to eject the shell cases
to drive nuclear power stations
and let off fireworks
of human imagination

Some reactions however resist utilisation
and so some thirty-five years after Hiroshima
the ammunition dumps the world over hold
thousands of nuclear warheads and bombs
And more than thirty years after our Victorious February
there is an alarmingly rapid growth
of new parasites

Every action produces a reaction
I'm not and never shall be a millionaire
with my poetry and my organisations
I am dead serious about this
But not about contraception

As evidenced by your new
expectant-mother card
And as betrayed by your swelling belly
in which a nameless Blanik saviour-knight
still slumbers

I know you are not well
And I'm not easy either
but I believe – though we are unbelievers –
that when we both feel worst
the mountain will open up and our little knight
armoured in his own delicate skin will with a loud scream peremptorily
        command
    – All enemies of love,
    let their heads be chopped off!

Ohm's Law

The condition for the emergence of an electric current
is an electric tension
created between the positive and negative
poles of the source
But different conductors offer the current
a different resistance
And hence the same voltage will produce
in different conductors
a different current
$I = V/R$
A poem is born between the positive and negative poles
of poet and reader
reason and heart
And its strength depends
on the magnitude of tension that arises
between their experiences
and their ability to generalise them
But the conductors offer it a natural resistance
and that's why editors delete
over-bold metaphors
and comparisons

Love is born of the tension
between the poles represented by
man and woman
between the poles of loneliness and someone's proximity
But resistance is offered to it by convention
fears for one's personal comfort
by distance   clothes   letters
and poor telephone lines
$R = V/i$
A conductor's resistance of course increases with its length
and decreases with its cross-section
It's much the same as with a good idea
which prospers where it finds
an open door
but which is jeopardised
by long journeys
endless authorisation tribunals
patent commissions
and trial runs

$V = I \times R$

The tension between us likewise
slowly increases day by day
as my love for you increases
as our resistance to obligations increases
and to all kinds of un-freedom generally

If things continue like this
it won't be long
before it's dangerous for us
to touch even poems
fallen to the ground

The Law of Inertia

A body continues in a state of rest or uniform rectilinear motion
unless compelled by external forces to change its state.

A tree continues existing in the forest until
human hand forces it
to fall on its knees
A rock continues in its place
until it's crumbled to gravel
by dynamite
The earth continues in its elliptical orbit
the sun at the centre of the solar system
the glass of wine on the table
the old gentlemen in the Chairs of history
motorcars on the roads
and armament shares on fluctuating markets

And yet it takes so little
to raise the glass to one's lips
to abolish the Chairs
Step on the brakes or lift the receiver
or trigger off a sufficient number
of nuclear bombs
And everything's totally different

The first of Newton's laws of motion
applies to all bodies
And humans are no exception
I've often realised it
on my own skin
Whenever someone's helping hand
lifted me off the ground or when
the celestial highway patrol stopped me
just when I felt
like some enormous star

External forces clearly are our fate
At one time it is pressure
to which we bend

Another it's a pull
to which we yield
And then again it's friction which gradually
slows down our flight
to new galaxies

Among those forces is contentment
weariness   yearning   also loss of faith
rejection of a manuscript
or some official measure
(performed invariably from a worm's eye's view)
a letter ending with
a signature and the words
    – Goodbye
      And don't ever
      expect me back

External forces however can also release us
from excessive calm
smoothly-running boredom
They can push us
upward towards our goal

And under this heading fall all revolutions
(in history one has never been enough)
enthusiasm and the wish to leap over one's shadow
heart transplants
head trepanations
reform manifestos and all high-risk
operations
pregnancy
declarations of love

External forces in point of fact include ourselves
who leave the warm nests of our families
and then screen our own dreams
in defiance of all laws and blind definitions
in colour on the black-and-white
television news

The Law of Mixture

Some substances can be mixed
with relatively good results
and others can be mixed
only with difficulty
And others yet cannot be mixed
or only at the risk
of an explosive mixture being created

Wine can be mixed with water
but blood only with blood
of another suitable donor
While firedamp can be mixed
with air only up to a certain limit
after which you find yourself
in the critical area of explosion

Under very similar circumstances
black can be mixed with white
rich with poor
and truth with falsehood
All up to a certain limit
a certain critical point

It is an afternoon in December
and the Davis Cup is on television

Panatta is playing Složil
and I am reflecting on
the definition of classes
which Marx began but never finished

Within a mere three months my second son
or a future daughter will probably be born
yet I don't know in what kind of a world
they'll come to live
A class-divided world
and a racially intolerant one

or in a world in which
man's ancient dreams and hard reality
will painlessly mix

The law of nature has not yet been formulated
and I cannot pretend to be able
to do so myself
And so I mix my faith with a touch of scepticism
And so I add some love to my hates
a little light to darkness
and to discipline at least
an occasional slight revolt

And when I am compelled one day
to mix my life
with the lives of all who have passed on
When I blend with that multitude
that is mixed with time
Do not forget that strictly speaking I
am always with you

My blood with yours in our children's blood
my steps with yours in the garden and in the house
our voices in our silences   our sentences   our words
which die away in the radio's background noise
in the monotonous drumming of railway wheels
in the clatter of all pistons and all typewriters
in the hiss of steam and in the autumn wind
and in the pick-up of the gramophone
which jumps
just as your voice did on the telephone
when I asked you
if you would like to live with me

The Law of the Conservation of Energy

Just think of all the energy I've put
into my poetry
And all the energy I've wasted
on my loves
Instead of giving my ability and strength
to my studies and to the job
that I am paid for

It's now mid-March and this year's winter
has long been one of those six-week pre-maternity leaves
But you're still in the maternity ward
and our spring is not yet tapping
even at our window
Meanwhile only red bottles of conserved blood
are winking like control lights
on the command panel of our love
comprising two hundred and sixty days

Our Monte Carlo Rally started
in July of last year
The first few miles we drove
on coastal roads and mountain hairpins
of Venus's isle of Cyprus
But now we're approaching the final bend
in Londýnská Street in Prague's district of Vinohrady
And we can't even rule out the possibility
that someone moves the finish back
to the Regional Maternity Centre or the Bulovka Hospital
or that he cuts the tape with a scalpel
of a caesarian

But you must endure it all
You are my wife and I never deceived you
that it would be an easy role
No energy is ever lost or created
Yours is transferred into the body
of our son
And mine
scattered among hundreds of embraces and thousands of words

will perhaps conserve its ability to transmit
feeling and thoughts over great distances

Maybe somewhere else
maybe in some other time
it will warm up another blind video screen

I lost a lot of friends
because of my red convictions
But maybe not even the energy
I invested in them
will be entirely wasted
Maybe they'll find a kind word for someone else
Maybe they'll help someone else when he's in trouble

I don't need anybody's help at the moment
but I don't believe I could manage forever
without somebody's help

Energy is neither lost nor created
Mechanical is merely converted into heat and vice-versa
hydraulic energy drives the turbines of our power stations
and electrical energy sets the early trains
of the Metro in motion

Energy gives rise to love and work
without which I would scarcely be able to feed
you and my children

Maybe what I'm saying is beginning to be incoherent
But tell me how am I to concentrate
when the last few yards of the Rally
are handled by you without me and all my energy
is of no use to you

I'd so much like to be with you
And that's why I'm writing this
accumulator poem
into which I'm crowding all
my energy
which should be converted
for yourself and for other
creatures great and small

The Law of Independent Motion

*If a body performs two or more motions simultaneously its resultant
position is the same as if it performed those motions consecutively
and in any sequence whatever.*

First I went to school and fishing and dancing
later to work   to meetings   to labour brigades
And on all these I spent
a lot of time
And only because I never really was any good
at physics

Today I realise that all these movements
or at least the most important of them
could have been performed simultaneously
and time saved

Think where I might now be
if I had always performed all my movements
at the right moment
and with the right people!

But now I know Galileo's law
I know my time is getting less
and my goals are retreating
like the lights at the back of the train
in a Metro tunnel shortly after midnight

I won't ride to the final station in a comfortable carriage
I can't get through the paper in the time
But I can in the course of a long nocturnal walk
drink a beer or buy
a hot dog for my Muse
I can write a poem
work out my salary
or meet one
of my former loves

Galileo's law has its champions
whose feats I can hardly hope to equal
because I never want to learn from them
Like during the love act acquire a gift
from someone or at least some valuable information
I do not desire the skill of during dinner
signing a warrant of arrests or an indictment
dictating a speech while sitting in an aircraft
or shaking hands while
looking at the camera

My eighteen-months-old daughter wakes me with her howling
from a nightmarish dream of high efficiency
at the hour when windows just as souls
sweat with anxiety and misty condensation
And I still bleary-eyed stare at my sheet of paper
No metaphors occur to me
no fissile rhymes and no
great thoughts

My yesterday was made up of reflection
of chopping firewood   of gutting a fish
of talking to my daughter   quarrelling with my wife
of a few lines of poetry   a few promises
short-lived as ephemeral flies above the water

The trout are beginning to rise again
The first birds are heard cheeping in the branches
The bats are slowly fading into the darkness
I have a back-ache   And I have trouble breathing
I cannot live by your law
clever Galileo
who it is now believed never really said
— And yet it moves
Even though without doubt you thought so
all your life

The Law of Force

A body's acceleration is in direct proportion to the
accelerating force and in inverse proportion to its mass.

At one time I very nearly stopped
in the same spot
At one time I very nearly turned to stone
from forever looking back
like Lot's wife

After all I had some certain things in life
Two rooms   a kitchen   a car   a position
mistresses and children
I had no need to hurry anywhere
Everything had its proper place
its time and reason
I knew when my daughter would graduate from school
when I'd get a salary rise
and at what age I'd be retired
There were few variables
and even fewer unknown quantities
And I felt no particular desire
to determine them

But then you came
Or perhaps I came and you were waiting for me
As the Magnetic Mountain in the Arabian Nights
was waiting for Sinbad the Sailor
and other unfortunate mariners

In short you upset my state
You imparted to me an initial acceleration
which enabled me to overcome
the attraction of old and routine affairs
Thus I lost my flat   my car and a carpet
I had to get used again
first to the public privacy of bedsitters
and then to new relations
and to new children's crying
But in return I gained a new view

of my own flaws
and also a new zest for life
Yes I am putting on weight again
(Small wonder considering
what passes through my stomach!)
Yet your accelerating force is not weakening
but on the contrary

I call this therefore a steadily accelerated motion
I am gaining speed every day
I iron nappies   shop for baby food
chase from pillar to post to get a new flat assigned to me
write articles   attend public meetings
and read the parliamentary reports

Poetry isn't dead but the sexual revolution
has been crushed

I delete from my diary all unnecessary meetings
I cancel dinner appointments already made
I disconnect the phone   throw away the addresses of all friends
I have no time   I have no time

If I die of cancer at age sixty
my youngest daughter will only be twenty-two
If I die of a heart attack at fifty
she'll be not quite thirteen
And if I kill myself in the car
tomorrow   next week or in a month
she'll know me only from some photographs
and from whatever some day
remains after me

I'll never reach the velocity of light
I'll hardly therefore
shine for her all her life
But if I could even sometimes serve
as an emergency light
I shan't have been here entirely in vain
my near and distant ones
whom I can only partly
recall by name

Michal Černík

Lines by way of a Prophecy

I have been late with everything.
With my first love, my first published book –
and now at forty I'll be a first-time father.
My wife will soon release her bequest to the world.
Her joy and mine will be muted
by fear for our child's future.
It's coming into a world that may destroy itself.
Meanwhile we're combing the calendar for a name for the one
who'll carry our blood and our hopes,
perhaps my wife's fire and perhaps my silent rebellion,
who'll inherit our Slav skulls and high foreheads,
our Slav souls and our unstable health,
our thinking, upbringing and customs,
who'll inherit this earth and sky
just as we inherited them.
We are experienced enough to know
that it must not choke on our emotions.

I believe that we'll be a good roof over its life.
It should be a daughter,
to protect us from the waste land of old age.
Daughters are more loyal to love,
but heaven knows I may be wrong.
If it's a boy that's fine by me.
He'll probably grow up in this house where I grew up,
he'll probably climb up on its roof one day
just as I once did,
to discover from that height a land within a land.
I shall be old when he casts off the burden of our will
and becomes his own person.
I wish him an ordinary life
and that he may stand up to it as a human being.

Identification

Someone is missing here.
Could it be me?
Someone here doesn't believe me.
Could it be me?
Someone here's convincing me.
Could it be me?
Someone here's maligning me.
Could it be me?
Someone here loves me.
Could it be me?
Someone here cannot stand me.
Could it be me?
Someone here's cursing me.
Could it be me?
Someone here's calming me.
Could it be me?

Yes, they're all me.
I just can't get on with myself in peace.

*

From time to time
I fill in boxes in questionnaires
in calligraphic block letters
to make sure I'm legible
so they know who I am.
And so I live on record
in the files of the National Committee, the police,
the district military office, the Czech Writers' Union,
the personnel department of my firm,
with all the data about my person.
I am on record in every printed line
which unambiguously finds me guilty.

At my age
I still have a lot of opportunities
to live differently,
but I live just
as I think.
And it's my life that determines
the logic of my thought and action.

*

Ah yes, life's a fine thing
but you've got to be good at it,
one of my uncles used to declare solemnly
and drank himself to death.

I too at times feel like a kid just starting school.
I'm no good at saying the right thing,
I'm no good at saying what I don't think,
I'm no good at converting my smile into a useful smile,
I'm no good at being clever, witty, important, obsequious,
I'm no good at making money
or building a career like a house.
I'm no good at noisy joy.
I tell myself: Joy soon passes.
I'm no good at noisy grief.
I tell myself: Grief too evaporates.
Out of a hundred things I'm not really good at any.
I can't even love with the same tenderness
as I did first so many years ago.
Maybe I'm no good even at crying.
I shan't be any good even at dying.
But that doesn't bother me.

I believe that I'm not anyone else
and therefore have no need to turn myself into someone else.
I live without hurrying, quietly, but so
as not to waste myself,
and I prefer life's marvellous gifts
to everything I'm no good at
and never will be.

*

A word on its own doesn't mean anything
until we fill it with the vigour of our lives,
until we feel in it the pulse-beat of our age
like that of our own hearts.

*

Much of my poetry is used as evidence against me
by my enemies
and as evidence in my favour
among my friends.
Pardon them if you will
or sentence them to death,
I won't be different.

Leave me some water to drink
and I will drink.
Leave me some water to wash
and I will wash.
Leave me some water to gaze at
and I will gaze at it.
Leave me some water to drown myself in
and I'll swim across.
I feel within myself a kind of rebellion
as still as water –
but I won't be still.

*

By writing
I'm learning to think
and to shape myself and others.

But I write less and less.
Just as if every poem
was to be the last ever.
What price the immortality of human creation!
I believe in creation
that gives meaning to life,
even if it's one single life.
It is the destiny of everything
to come to fruition and to an end.

Just like this poem. For a little while it will guard my name.
But that's not important now.
I'm trying to be happy
and find it can be done.

*

I didn't come into this world
to answer questions
about how am I,
or to ask in return
and how are you.
I lack the elegance of outward courtesies,
a sense of social banalities and decorum,
and so I tell myself I have a noble mind.
I hope there's something in it.

Ask me
why I am not caught up in the system of bribery and nepotism,
why so many have fashioned an armour out of the ideas of socialism,
why we make so many vacuous speeches and hold vacuous meetings,
why our thinking is being fashioned towards the next war,
why we must soil our hands each time we do a deed,
why I wish to add my trivial actions to that great action,
why I am not indifferent to what so many are indifferent to.
The world has reached a point
where I must give an answer.

*

I cannot live without friends
and I don't live without enemies.
If you wish to be true to yourself
it's bound to be against someone.

Our age requires no gestures.
The great hero figures are the stuff of legends.
I look for the logic in every action
and am inclined to back the kind of courage
that springs from a cool head and from conviction.

*

As I grow older
the boundaries of my privacy are shrinking.
I still have some options of what I can do
but there are things now which I must do.
My only time for lyrical moods is in the intervals.
I point my finger and a shot rings out.
That shot does not come out of my finger
but somewhere it kills someone.
Reality has alarmingly hardened.

I didn't choose this age
nor this country,
but no matter what they're like
they accepted me as theirs
and I can't remain in their debt.
I've got to build up what I have,
and prove I exist.
I'm not leaving any fairy-tale behind me.
I have no need to shine
to be seen,
but to shine
so there is light.

*

So far I haven't sobbed with happiness
nor gone insane with love,
I never suffered like an animal,
never fell victim to despair,
never was sentenced to a different fate,
and human infamy I only knew by hearsay.
Ask me what wish I have
and I'll reply: to be happy.
Ask me if I am happy
and I'll reply: So far.
I've a good job and a good wife
and nothing to complain about.
The worst may happen any moment.
I want to be strong.

Sometimes I talk of death
because I think of life.
And living means rebellion,
never to be a humble sheep
nor a wolf.

Working Poem

Even the fact you are never seen at your place of residence
is being held against you, my friend,
it'll go on your personal file.
You should at least attend your residents' meetings.
No one, after all, is interested
in the fact that you spend all your time working
and relax only when you are asleep,
and sleep so little.
Less is expected of you
than you expect of yourself,
and more is demanded of you
than you can meet
in terms of your work-place duties
and your public activities,
which you have still not managed to harmonise
with your private life and your writing of poetry.
Sometimes you're haggard with fatigue,
sometimes you'd like to finish some book you've started reading,
sometimes you need to be idle for a few days or a few hours,
but it seems you no longer know how.

Conferences, seminars, teach-ins, committees,
report-backs, planning, evaluation, meetings
often suffer from a congestion of vacuous big-mouths.
A subject needs to be addressed clearly and factually
or else our chairs become our pedestals.
Work's your salvation and your real life.
I'm in the same boat, mate.
We both know that words exist
to serve and not to be subservient.

To start a race all you need is a pistol,
to order an attack all you need is a coloured flare,
to express praise all you need is applause or a handshake.
Even a fist-blow is eloquent enough.
Here we don't need words and I'm not going
to make a speech when I've nothing to say.
I'd like to write an ode to celebrate work,
except that I don't like songs of praise.
But I do believe that we won't forget how to work,
I believe that without sweat there's no bread,
I believe that work is the mother of progress,
I believe that work ennobles man.
To believe means to get hold of life and make it bright.

Short Essay on Fools

Names do not matter.
Fools are anonymous.
Their existence is proved by nonsensical prohibitions.
They have a remarkable gift
for creating a resistant state of matter
and their eager application has always buried
all revolutionary ideas and roads to progress.
In history they perform an important function,
even though history records no famous fools.
The fools are the guardians of all dead truth,
the creators of darkness.

And when that darkness was pierced by light
it was the light of fire
consuming books,
the bodies of John Huss and Giordano Bruno.
Fools are more dangerous than enemies
whom we know to be facing us.
They'll be our friends so long
as we are strong.
Even fools sometimes can say something sensible,
but that's no reason to applaud them.
We have no law that would protect us from them.

I'm neither the Beginning nor the End

A thousand years people have thought for me,
worked for me, created for me,
suffered for me, had pleasure and made love
under the ever-present supervision of death.
A thousand years people have overcome obstacles for me,
overcome even themselves,
either to triumph or to be vanquished.
That was their task in history,
a task as natural as life itself.
A thousand years people were born for me and died again.
No guardian angel hovered above their heads,
protecting them against all evil, not even against themselves,
repeating the miracle that had already happened:
that they were born, that they were alive,
and thus were exhausting their only chance,
having to rely on themselves alone.
A thousand years I was getting ready to be born.
And here I am,
so I too can exhaust my only chance,
so I can spend myself and give my all,
so I can fulfil myself as a human being
and become a bequest just as a child is the bequest of a woman.

This word to which I listen
is my name.
This flesh and blood are my body,
which I drag around with me everywhere
and introduce by my name.
This poem I am writing
is my fragment.
This daily routine I'm living
is my destiny.
This life I own
is my introduction to death.
My death will be my own death alone
and I'll no longer be I.

We're all in the same boat.
We start each new day in our beds.
We cannot manage without joy or sadness,
we cannot manage without love or love-making,
None of us ever reflects
that we weren't here before,
but are terrified we soon won't be here.

Everything's OK on the whole, I tell myself,
so long as every day has its tomorrow and next time,
its joys and its hopes
and its pain of delight like the seasons of the year,
so long as man hasn't lost control of himself
and time past and time future are within one day.
Life's thought me up for a few decades
and I am neither its beginning nor its end.

Deformation of Logic

Nature wasn't equally generous to everyone.
The clumsy tortoise it protected by an armour, the snake's soft body by
poisonous fangs,
the little lark by camouflage colouring,
the helpless gazelle it equipped with speed,
the ant with organisational talent, the flea with parasitism,
to the ephemera it gave just one day's life,
to man it gave the power of reasoning
and so he invented the means of killing.
Today mankind can kill itself sixteen times over,
while conducting summit talks
on reducing its war potential,
so it can kill itself only five times over.
I'll never understand the logic of such death.
To die just once is quite enough for me.

The Treaty

Gelon, the ruler of Gela and Syracuse in Sicily
was waging war against the Carthaginians.
When he'd defeated them his only demand was
that they give up their custom of sacrificing little children.
Clearly this was the finest peace treaty
since the victors' conditions benefited the vanquished.
That was two and a half thousand years ago
and even then it was quite out of keeping
with the custom of victors
and ripe for legend.

The Suicide Tree

In the Amazonian jungle there grows a curious tree.
If it is badly wounded it will writhe in spasms,
tear out its roots from the ground and crash down dead.
The people call it the Suicide Tree.
Is it its will or some command of nature
that shares out life and death
evenly among all living things?
Some ancient law
assigns to some the strength to live
and to others faint-heartedness.
That's how it was, and is, and will be.
And that's why I admire
the tiny birch seed:
caught in the crevice of a medieval wall
it will unfold into a tree.

Photographers' Models

I possess a calendar with delightful nudes
modelling jewellery on their naked bodies.
The first sits, legs slightly apart, on a baroque sofa.
Her lips are sensually open
and her glance is provocatively inviting:
Come on, let's fill that empty bed with our bodies,
let's devastate it with our ecstasies!

It's all part of their job.
They're objects for men's eyes to feast on.
From the moment of their pose
to this day some twenty years have gone.
Life's repossessed itself of all their charms
and this bright piece of paper's all that's left
of vanished beauty.

That fragile, delicate human body!
The soul wants love,
the body another body,
and we who're animally active do not know
whether we love a woman only for our own sake
because we love her body
that gives us bliss...

*

It's a long time since I last wrote a love poem
I seemed to be seeking verbal substitutes
for what a man and woman can say only while making love.
While making love no word is ever too much.
Too much is only the moment when we dress again.

Karel Sýs

The Time Machine

The Time Machine

The first bars of music on a record are fingered
rubbed or skipped
as an uncaring fate has run a nail or a file over it
And just as difficult is it to start a poem
Words too are fingered or rubbed
before they start running
like a fateful letter finally dropped in the mail-box
Nowhere does a man feel more lonely than in Paris
Isaac Babel wrote
That's why it is a good idea to start this poem here
for it was in this city that you were eaten through with longing
like the Louis Quinze furniture
Not even you my son
my fair-haired little beacon-light
can reach as far as this
to the Porte de Clignancourt
where I'd show you the flea market
You reel – a pierced cork
on the surface of undamaged ones
You want to be exact in this chaos
but to be exact means to be dead
Remember the platinum-iridium metre
kept at Sèvres not far from here
In love up to your ears
you're waiting for a letter or at least a telegram: Ahasverus
The Black Peter of adults
You float on an ice-floe on a hot ocean
round the Hachette publishing house
round the Cape of Disappointed Childish Hope
Compelled to pay for everything in hard currency
In the heart's refrigerator winter is settling in
purple like rings under your eyes
You're hungry while out of Greek restaurants
asparagus and crab sauce flow on to the pavement
It's exhausting to feed by sniffing greasy flowers
You suck the autumn smell as a child sucks
a herb-drenched crimson nipple
The bubble of Burgundy has burst
and the juice of drunken wrath rises
into the grapes as they turn blue

Girls lithe and educated cross the street
with eyes ruined by reading
a veil of flint-glass drawn over them
You gobble up their underwear
a harvester reaping lace
(Mouth watering with sex)
Oh, to pass them neatly from hand to hand
like a pair of lovers squeezing their hands in Dobříš
wearing the most delicate locally-made gloves
You make for rue Saint-Denis
that meeting place of mucous membranes
The girls in the peep-show keep changing like rings during
        show-of-hand voting
always one ruby between two gleaming white opals
and in the cabins a hot white coat runs over the men's hands
You call out to them: I am Christ
a rubber virgin
Women will accept just one on the cross
but here there's a whole row of them
You're suddenly reminded of St Matthew's fair
At the base of the sphere of death stands a girl in black stockings
while her father up in the dome is riding around her
the small hairy motorbike of my glances
rides round her upright thigh
Who'll give what sustenance
to a heart like mine?
Noon in Christina Street
'Do not disturb your wife while she is having an orgasm!'
'Is a closer acquaintance possible?'
'If he has never smoked so far
why should he now light a cigar?'
'Those are improper associations'
'I want to be sick'
'Have you ever seen the inside of an airship
the skeleton, the ropes and wires?
And that's nothing compared to your inside
and doubly nothing
compared to your fate's chassis!'
'She didn't know what she wanted
gave herself airs and turned one man down after another
until outside the students' hostel
a Number 21 ran her over
A piece of kidney was still lying there in the evening'

'All is nothing
only God's stick poking into emptiness'
'He found a 3 + 1 at Père Lachaise'
'I'd sooner have a bachelor flat in Olšany'

*

Suddenly you long for a human soul
as if you were the only man in the Silurian
Rimbaud – if he were alive – that is only freeze-dried
or instant
You'll never forget the hymn to Apollinaire
sung by a choir of old maids from the Abbey of Saint-Germain
A-A-Apollinaire
Then with Jiří Žáček we cross-lace Saint-Germain
I'll bet the boulevard's sandal was never laced so tight
Bohemian regions, oh, how sad you are and joyless
But you can't fall asleep
Instead of counting sheep
you try to name all the streets in Písek
Thus you struggle through the night
old and older yet now by another night
You rock like a trunk on a train like a drawn pheasant
Oh once more to drink
that Bzenec wine – the Czech Chablis
or else Tramiener
curative and dry
a walnut ground to an edge

*

Space and time
are but two gloves
put on the same hand
and therefore can be easily interchanged
To make the world as small as possible
and not as big as possible
that is the joke
This is the question

*

Do you feel that fate is grinding you too much
in its agate mortar?
Does your stomach turn as it does in the lift
of the White Swan department store?
Do you want to return before the cause of the effects?
Do you want to take it in one fell swoop?
Step out of the treadmill?
Please do!
The world is terrible
Yes
But why should we poets take the rap for it?
Are we confessors or large-capacity confessionals
janitors or block representatives
family doctors friends and psychiatrists
hawk-eyes ex officio
jacks and janes-of-all-trades
puffed with authority
philanthropists and grasses
bringers of luck chimney-sweeps four-leaved clovers
saxifrage and common sundew
aloes amulets rabbits' feet philosophers' stones?

*

You spend the night combing the ether
fingering the long waves
playing with the curls of VHF
The world's growling at itself
the ionosphere is barking and it bites
Poet you put it right!
Figaro here Figaro there
Figaro fast Figaro slow
Figaro come Figaro go
You all rely on poetry as a sedative
Sleep softly
as Bohemia that baroque Bohemia under the snow
You whistle and someone else
is working for your salvation
your happiness
maybe cutting not a Christmas tree
down in the forest but his throat
like Jakub Jan Ryba

*

You who will straighten even the corner
of a turned-up carpet
because you believe that the molecules perceive and lament
scarcely believe that humans can be treated
like chunks of discarded meat on a butcher's slab
It's x years since the war   The ozone has oxidised
the blood the urine sweat and tears on Terezín's walls
a breeze is rustling in the fortress passages
but no White Lady haunts them now
It's hard to think that under this throb of engines
the ramps of Peenemünde were once shaking
or that there was such busy traffic
on the selection ramps of Auschwitz
You and your children's train goes only to known destinations
Veleslavín Buštěhrad Lidice are left behind
Nothing is dark here but your glasses
because the sun is scorching documents are yellowing
they are as yellow now as the stars in the museum
The prisoners' rags look more and more like the pyjamas
of mythical sleepers who have long since gone
You're choking – mentally at least – on milk and juice and honey
and now the curly flocks of sheep rush out
cow-eyed Achaeans will be herding them
herding and playing shawms Achaeans and Czechs
And Říp will urge you on
to set breasts swinging rather than bells
Today's bells cannot even scare midday
When in the sky a flight
of spluttering fighters whistles past
like spitting in a child's bowl

*

We lie down in our cots in fact subtenants
strange arms are hugging us
hands not observing Sunday
My son your little hand gleams in my hand like a nugget
I attach myself to it like an intensive care unit
Your little heart is beating for me your liver and kidneys are rustling
     for me
Hush like a dormouse so mummy doesn't find us
I burrow into the pillow like into a dream
like this the doomed awaited the Gestapo

But nothing's threatening us
for this is January 1982
We are surrounded by care and by warmth
In Northern Bohemia some unknown people are not observing Sunday
and are pulling hot chestnuts out of the mud for us
And the thought that winged missiles
are swotting up their flight-paths by heart
paths which intersect our flat as well
is laughable

*

Take a deep breath and go by train
is Josef Rybák's ironic pun
on my book Take a deep breath and fly
He knows how scared I am of flying
On Moscow airport at the sight of a child's sword
from the GUM department store I nearly burst into tears
Suppose the plane crashed and you couldn't dig yourself out my
          small son
Since then I have been crawling close to the ground
I missed Montreal India and longed-for Abyssinia
Rimbaud's Harar
I never saw Mongolia or Helsinki
nor Irish towns fenced in by armistice
By now they won't even send me to some two-horse dump
And yet I honour Orville Wright above the patriarch Jacob complete
          with ladder
But I'm aware that the greatest invention of all time is central heating
because total strangers are hugging and warming us in cast-iron arms
And that is love
greater than the love of all heavenly choirs
because we the Unchosen do not call out: Father why hast thou
          abandoned me
but: Lord why didn't you heat our homes?

*

I'm like an angel under the hairdresser
a wicked hairdresser
a vicious barber
My face is laid waste
My halo is fading
because I'm slowly running out of gas...

'Well then, poet Sýs
how're things?
That pen of yours – deserting you?'
'Deserting me all right, even in this desert it's deserting me'
Can't make an omelette even if you break the blown-out painted
        Easter eggs!
Some filthy swine keeps phoning you
breathing heavily and listening
to your breathing and hanging up
You're small fry, too small for them to waste even a symbolic bullet
        on you
Nothing that happens to you now will be without pain
Like some toothed Christ you drag behind you a tail of eternal brides
more ruins in your wake than walls
Leporello and Don Giovanni at the same time
The file K.S. is not yet closed
He regularly saw this person or that
He slept here and there
The mercury of his actions hasn't reached
the mark: Accomplished
Even so there are plenty of those who'd like to know
even Homer's ID number

*

After midnight the flat shrinks down to a table and chair
like Jean-Paul Sartre's apartment
when he stopped buying books
after the Secret Army had blown his library sky-high
And the only ornament in the room
is the moral law in the sky
and the infinity of stars in your soul

*

It's spring the time of heatwaves is approaching
the time of open windows evenings on balconies
People are hurrying to summer lodges and cottages
to inhale resin hay iodine
And you are hurrying to your typewriter
you're yourself a machine
a machine for articles book reviews
short bits of news for 35 Crowns apiece

a machine for cutlets steaks and liver
which you can't stand but which you have to stand for
in queues outside the butcher's at St Peter's
the former Jewish ritual butcher's shop
Once Christian girls were hung there by their legs
today it's legs of pork and best of neck
You'd like to be a playboy but it is too late
You can barely sit down in trousers made for you to measure a mere
        month ago
You drag your belly with you
as an astronaut does his life-support pack
You're turning into a capon Al Capone
a machine for tea from the Duty Free Shop
because that shop is a great poet and has written a beautiful poem
Orange Pekoe Darjeeling Earl Grey
Your days are free-falling towards December
like the blood of a calendar supplied in January
No for the dream life I am not the kind
The magician's gone he's left his tricks behind
Hush, death knell, hush
I know that thought too well
At least, God, hurl me down on Jupiter

*

I've seen the best brains of my generation
writhe in the jaws of a career
37 years after the last war
and my own brain too
You can buy anything you like
But when did you last lie in the grass?
When did you last bake in the sun
without asking: how much does this grill cost?
Happiness isn't a golden fly it's a bluebottle hovering above a rotten
        memory
But we must build a new happiness
Come let's break down this cage
We won't be afraid of the wolf time anything
I don't want to see the best brains of my generation
spread out dove-grey
under the attic beams of "post-war" Europe
squashed like a dog mess outside the Metro at rush hour

*

They're telling us:
'Don't dig your gardens
leave off that bricklaying when completion can't be guaranteed
why should you give a damn
they won't give you either fruit or shade
roofs won't protect against that kind of rain
What will be after the war?
I'll tell you in 45 minutes'

*

We belong to those who remember crabs in the waters
who're still amazed by the bustle of metal in the air
those who can say: my grandad had a shop
in the days when ancient trees were not cut down
but Chinese lanterns hung among the branches
Flies would descend on them not killed by sprays yet
Ah those trees which sheltered swarms of fireflies
The tar at the bathing place smelled like the South
and the story of Romeo and Juliet was so exciting
when you inhaled the scent of the forbidden froth on beer
Uncle
do you remember how you pulled out the plug in the deep water
and the boat's soul and mine began to escape
and so I can say: yes I was drowned
But I never reconciled myself to its not happening again.

*

You all think:
he's grown old
he's developed a paunch
never does anything but laze about
And instead I'm falling backward into childhood
Another moment – if all goes well –
and I shall smell camomile and the tar on the underside of the boards
at the swimming baths
Until suddenly I discover
that although childhood is possible down below
I'm warming myself like a down-and-out
shut off from it by the sewer grill

Yes I am old
I have a paunch
a back bruised by cast-iron and no wings
Nirvana is firmly fenced in

*

I sink my teeth into a summer apple
and the film of my life
starts running backward
An ordinary film no Paramount
no Twentieth Century Fox

*

Behold I'm in the garden with little Annie
at the centre of gravity of the universe
through my teeth bursts the torrent of my first declaration of love
till it re-echoes among the redcurrants: I love you
It is my turning point
Behold Annie's hair honey dropped from a plane on a bed of
      marguerites
Behold her armpits a mortar for grinding haematite and pepper
Behold I'm riding a motorbike the thread's unwinding backwards
Behold through half-open doors the past is rushing in
Behold silence broken only by the clock's stampede
The stampede of a herd of elephants mating in the china shop
Behold this poem: it has no end
The poem that ensures time's savage heat
will see not you, but the poem – your faithful counterfeit
Behold the poem – a wound...